THE UPSTATE

s de Nueva España de Úrsula Camba Ludlow
e terminó de imprimir en octubre de 2022
en los talleres de
Impresora Tauro, S.A. de C.V.
Año de Juárez 343, col. Granjas San Antonio,
Ciudad de México

PHOENIX POETS

Edited by Srikanth Reddy

Rosa Alcalá, Douglas Kearney &

Katie Peterson, consulting editors

The Upstate

LINDSAY TURNER

THE UNIVERSITY OF CHICAGO PRESS

CHICAGO & LONDON

The University of Chicago Press, Chicago 60637
The University of Chicago Press, Ltd., London
©2023 by The University of Chicago
Published 2023
Printed in the United States of America

32 31 30 29 28 27 26 25 24 23   1 2 3 4 5

ISBN-13: 978-0-226-82864-0 (paper)
ISBN-13: 978-0-226-82865-7 (e-book)
DOI: https://doi.org/10.7208/chicago/9780226828657.001.0001

Library of Congress Cataloging-in-Publication Data

Names: Turner, Lindsay, author.
Title: The upstate / Lindsay Turner.
Other titles: Phoenix poets.
Description: Chicago : The University of Chicago Press, 2023. | Series: Phoenix poets
Identifiers: LCCN 2023000622 | ISBN 9780226828640 (paperback) | ISBN 9780226828657 (ebook)
Subjects: LCGFT: Poetry.
Classification: LCC PS3620.U76557 U67 2023 | DDC 811/.6—dc23/eng/20230113
LC record available at https://lccn.loc.gov/2023000622

⊚ This paper meets the requirements of ANSI/NISO Z39.48-1992 (Permanence of Paper).

for my father

It was not regional it was systemic.

C. D. WRIGHT

CONTENTS

THE UPSTATE

Planning

Once there was an image of a garden projected on a screen
Once there were orderly hedges and white gravel paths
The garden wasn't planned for getting lost in but that's what people did there
It was just the garden's outlines but you could still trace the paths
It's not at all like how the straight line of history (now we know)
Runs out in the depopulated suburbs where the wires run aboveground
Runs out in strip malls, parking lots of trailers selling pills and armchairs
Runs out in a wealth of places of supplies for everything mechanical or animal

Once I couldn't wait a moment longer in Virginia
Once the sun rose red outside a hotel room in the cold New England dawn
I couldn't imagine any other way to sleep I hadn't tried
Cocooned inside one form or another

Why doesn't anyone in these poems speak for her own life
Once I wasn't thinking about the running out
Once I wasn't thinking about anyone else's life or mine as such
I imagined my arm extending outside the window in the cold red morning
Held there in the cold red like a steeple while the day rushed past

Is this when the poem appears like a crime scene
Like a white outline of smoke or breath in a red New England dawn
It's not an allegory in the strictest sense because the made-up part of it is true

Why doesn't anyone here speak for their own life
Once in South Carolina there was a flood behind the storage units
Once it was believed relief from was a thing in store
In my life the major errors accumulate behind me as I go
Soon you will be able to read them like a poem

The Upstate

It always was a little like an outpost here
The sun is big behind the smog
You fill out forms and then you die

The red bush looked like it felt to return to life
The dog came back with ticks on her face
Inside you're being all sorts of people

I cleaned so much and the sky was dark
It wasn't cold but it was damp enough
Have you forgotten what peripherals are

The trees glowed but it felt like the end of air
I cleaned so hard we could see the outlines
Then I fell asleep and woke up on the porch

When the leaves blew against the windshield
The volume was turned all the way down
If nothing works out, I guess you could just *volunteer* somewhere

There were animals with bloodied muzzles
The dog barked at all the cows in Virginia
Whatever kills us will be slow and from the inside

A coffee from the QuikTrip full of chemicals
The dry leaves on the floor in the hallway scared me
Maybe like love as it curled somewhere deep in the chest

The Upstate

this is now
the dark underbelly

dogfights in the mountain county where they found the dog beside the road
the edges turning yellow, strain in the house and over it

how could we and survive
living in the place I left by choice
living season when things are decided

learned care / learned care pushed past care

roadside goldenrod
season of contentment / of the beast

Overlook

this is now
the anxiety you never chose
in the mountains, mountain ash
find the verb for how you lost

in the mountains, mountain ash
red berries flashed out in dry brush
find the verb and suffer it
with someone else—

find the verb and suffer it
drove through where the paper mill
suffer the anxiety and the election
of the fools—

in the air the paper mill
released it all into the air
sunlight tangled in the air
and down the mountain—

has anyone checked up on the air
did you think you got to choose
does anyone ever get to choose
and still end up together

drove through mountains in the drought
suffer through the verb together
this is what you didn't choose
and what might outlast

Accomplice

like taking the leash in your teeth so to speak
acres on fire, walking the dog through a smudge
and breathing it deep

accomplice you said but what does it mean
is it that I would have chosen it but I did not
reading Arendt at the gym I dig deep
and would bury it all like a dog if I could

Forms of Displeasure

the hawks are a-nesting
storms in the evenings
no the hawks are re-nesting
the forest is gone

they clearcut the forest
the smell of black plastic
the forms of displeasure
are circling the lot

prescient bright winged things
big iridescent bubbles
the forms of displeasure
blow over like storms

what you need to understand is
it's big things not people
the bright formal nothings
go rising up the hill

it's things and not people
it's braided with pleasure
phthalates and parabens
circling like drones

what goes in the new space
like are you the new girl
like rotted out rope strands
the rope hollow at the core

The Upstate

bloodstain from the deer fanned out over the highway
sky every night in a brick-red October
over ditches and guardrails, over the front stoop

whooping and hollering into the evening
what miasma released from pipes into the air
brush pile on the curb with a pepper plant in it
the water's not clear so there's red in it too

red sky in the morning set out to warn you
what would a cent get you if you spent it
what would it take to get at the truth of it
the truth is what everything is when you squint

Tennessee Quatrains

what would it be like to stay here forever

we went up a mountain and went up a fire tower

the seasons themselves felt annulled like a marriage

it doesn't matter if it was never gone through with

to whom does the texture of a landscape matter

in the hero's landscape it gutters and shakes

the men put their hands wherever they want to

what kind of thing's hiding under this rock

heaven forbid you built by the creekside

what kind of mud understructures the house

in some cultures it's kept anecdotal

the singer lay down in the forms of her dress

what kind of thing stays away in the mountains

rain only exists in relation to need

sometimes the citizens quake in the mountains

a wash, and awash, and a-wash it away

New City

just at the moment when it was for sale
I wanted to cast a spell on it
not because it was so good
but to protect it from becoming what they advertised

just at the moment of coming soon
poised in the posture of being for sale
silver grass, maiden grass, red ground beneath
pretty blond planks then some days for the walls

welcome the new store selling you plants
mosquitoes and pipelines, conversational din
at the moment of tipping or not tipping
planted the birds are thousands these days

at the moment of peak growth, unexpected
the phone takes any voice and turns it to pieces
next spring, ten more minutes, it's almost done
a pile of bricks and grass growing from sod

Song of Accumulation

I was in another state when it happened
long since left out under the sky
I felt the glass grow lighter in my hand
I thought, I should pay more attention to what's strange

so long since out under the sky at night
some white streaks then just nothing
there's an office for change and there's one for savagery
you think "pristine" but it just means not yet accumulated

you think "pristine" but it just means uncluttered
like a new office where there isn't much junk yet
or how about we reverse that, afterward there'll be less

there was stubble in the field and a throat that rattled
out under the night sky shouting, "I hate men"
then there was less than stubble in the field
when the leaves blew away it was mostly mud

there was a yard but there was less than grass in it
when you say "less," please explain what you mean
in another state, an office for savagery

an office for change another for savagery
I was in another state, trying to get things done
there was less than stubble in the field and still something rattled
you think "possibility," please explain exactly what you mean

Spells & Charms

Premonition

reeds by the lake and the clay
two little swifts one over
one under the other
red clay / the day detests

hot light in the hot sky
haze and the light waits
to come down / particulate
the hot sky waits to get at us

Pretty Like That

beautifully they picnicked on the point of an island
named after kings swans or something
pretty like that

and the wind across plastic glasses sang a
raspberry almost froze the police in a rubber boat going fast
pretty like that

and then I walked home quick
whose neighborhood bliss of ignorance white glass traced side mirror smashed
pretty like that

The Upstate

now draw down the light of evening
there's a substance that the toxins want to claim and have
they put solutions straight into the bloodstream
before we knew I felt the silence fall

hold a silence in your hand or fight it
it felt like spring out on the decimated lawn
next thing you know they'll blur it all again
infusing everywhere like spring into the trees

the changes gather in the bloodstream and move out from there
the people gather shouting at the airports or are stuck there
the people gather somewhere or die trying
this is neither metaphorical nor new

the neighbors put some rocks across their driveway
in the trees the twigs arrange themselves, cascade
then there was this voice saying that men are animals
I felt that in the trees the twigs would soon explode

it's one thing to know what was in the bloodstream
I said I needed to be able to blame someone exactly
the pink light gathering beyond the screen, the porch, the frame
repository for the times you said and meant "I hate"

Charm for J

ruby, garnet, opal ring
what rescues you could lose its hold
the honeysuckle leaves went dark
pick a birthstone for the past

emerald, garnet, sapphire
every mothered creature leaves
that all the care of caring past
polished up, could hold you there

pearl or moonstone, peridot
who cares if the thing's a scam
nothing could be worse than time
except the time that came between

opal, ruby, garnet ring
humid summer will be past
say the heavy days are jewels
wear them like they're really jewels

Charm for W

sea glass, neoprene
a ring round the island
the ocean was up all night and all morning
the red things were rose hips
I had to look it up for you
the sun burns through, or not

golden fleece, bladder wrack
a kind of commitment
the sea by the seawall smelling like death
sugar kelp, sea silk
sun burn a space for you
lacy queen anne's lace and rockweed on rock

Charm for the Neighborhood

your shipment was delivered
in a thousand tiny boxes
filled with air and plastic
but what's the backyard like

hollyhock past blooming
green ferns with rusty fronds in them
anthill, rusty mushroom bulb
a leaf floats down to where it stays

Charm for G

pearl all night
yellow violence in the grass
I don't know how you could fight them

had a thought, lost it
don't take the debt they offer you
stabbed in the neck at the Regal Inn

in the yellow of the air
blisters from the new used shoes
what should be circling is circling

August you neurotic hallucination
at the top of the building, unrelated
that the sunset only be credible, credible

It Imagines the Destruction It Wants

That the next storm rip the faces off your pretty seaward-facing houses with their
painted- spindle porches

That each red paving brick be pried up by the wind or by the rocks or by the big
trees you will never claim for shade or silhouette

That your french doors blow out so hard they slam against the walls and shatter, that
not even the skeletons of french doors be left inside or outside the house

That the ground you fitted for the gates be stripped again of its green sod, unnamed
by you, removed beyond your measure

Vows

Tired of being found cold it was during a heat wave and I
A concert at which there were no white men
If not like that with force and multiple or not at all
Then her grandmother's white shell necklace broke on stage and was felt
Hotter now than Egypt and burning into straw
The streets scorched a few days like this every time there has been before
A comfort
Promise it will not be in our lifetimes that it turns to fire
Promise it will be a forgetting in some few years that we have felt like that before
This nothing new under the waiting around for it
An afternoon if I can't put it into
The wall a panel with the white light coming in anyway from underneath around the
Shade beneath which you are typing on your stomach
Into the sky with nothing nothing nothing in it
None of it original
A concert
A black swallow way up high
Nectar of beauty no it was gardens
Gardens of beauty on the table
In the gardens what was said there in the most convicted repetitions of convention
At least until the next age if it holds we want to until the next a hot white light and will be
                                                                    a more just one
Burning transparent all the way up to the top where the workers
Rise into a general collective of all they wouldn't offer

Superstition

red sky whenever
whatever the weather
red sky at all times
will all the rhymes fail

The Compass

crooked little smile moon—
I'm always the one pulled
or by you from the inside—

trepidation of the spheres, September
and everything hot and trembling, I mean
serious, grave, the land unanswerable beneath the haze—

by the time you landed on another continent
I'd been to sleep and back

Tender Publics

Midway or the midpoint of my life
I understood the need to decompress
There was never enough tenderness in texts
Storms rolled through every day for weeks
I drove through some of them

I drove through many strip malls on the way—it felt familiar
The sign said "window tinting" or "sunless tanning"
I drove through and forgot immediately
Along the way were many forms of tyranny
The mist rolled up the mountain as I drove

I rolled the window down and rolled it up again
I said, I can't take you a mile down the road
It was because he was he, not because he was poor
She ate her oatmeal like a much older woman
She furrowed her brow but it could no longer be furrowed
Chemicals and plastics make such differences

Closets and cabinets etc. make such differences
Everybody wants to give me a china set
No one in this life wants a china set
Oh just set her up in a house
No you can't even sell it

Oh I found us a red wooden house by a creek
I found us a white house with a vegetable garden already going strong
Oh I found us a kitchen of windows
I know I said I didn't want to go outside ever again
No but I did

Accomplice
(Isabella from *Measure for Measure*)

Isabella riding in a car with the boys
Isabella as the music to choose from formed by bruising against it
Isabella whole while whatever weather comes against the windshield

Isabella feeling safe and would you have to choose, Isabella,
then exchange it all for doom in the form of the police car
followed me to the hill, turned down it like a watershed—

the night hanging in the air like a purple hologram, you see,
Isabella, power is a real thing comes at you like a hologram
they hold it out metallic and agential, Isabella,

too much to imagine if you want to keep your warm hands warm
driving to high school and you park in the sky

or into an arms race where you could, Isabella,
strike at them when you pleased—but who
would let you, Isabella, steady

below the pink full of honeybees
the professor listening to old Italian patriotic hymns
all buzzy on his iPhone—at the end of the workday, winking

sinister, Isabella, there is actually a prohibition against you
being true in any of the worlds, a partition
sturdy in its gorgeous velvet glory

Just Work

called about what time for sunset
just to keep heads down to business / caught
in meshes of the post-op
just to keep it all in the washing

✳

just to keep someone constant and beside
aisles and aisles / lasts like some flowers
Food City bleak city blank city no city
if the road went flat it might run away

✳

oh five her fingers oh other fire
where the road goes white and shining
cast attention—as in iron—
just to keep someone bridal and beside

Wasted Empty Space

spring light on a cold tin roof
it happens when the seasons change
the body's molecules all rearrange—an itchy feeling—
you see the place as it has always been or

entirely monstrous! frost-killed glory
the people under the rug
the ants in constant streaming lines

the roads you couldn't dream of crossing
the close rhyme of *venal* and *vernal*
anyway, a little song to end on:

LITTLE SONG TO END ON

IF YOU HAD A HEADLAMP LIKE A MINER
IF YOU HAD AN EARTAG LIKE A COW
IF YOU HAD A SCHEDULE LIKE A MOTHER
IF YOU HAD A LIST OF FLOWERING TREES

Saucer Magnolia
Southern Magnolia
Sweet Bay
Crape Myrtle
Flowering Dogwood
Eastern Redbud

It's the Stupidest Thing

Good morning.
The yard is full of chokeweed
and stringy buttercups, suddenly.
There's a lot to want, badly.
It's the stupidest thing.
I'm a person who believes in the value of intelligence.
I'm in the Bi-Lo parking lot yowling at the daytime moon.
You've made your moves and now you have to lie there.
How long will it last?
Longer than this spring, now springing robustly.
The medium-big green leaves become a darkish tunnel.

Dogwood

The flat flowers looked a little childish
But I was grateful for their presence
Like you'd be grateful sometimes
If there were a child present.

In the dogwood the light collected.
Toothy notches in the petals
White as the sheets and pillowcases,
Of which the person I married had many.

Mostly I felt wounded,
Like there was a tiny stream of blood
Leaking but going back in
Before there was too much harm.

Rusty eye of the dogwood,
Pair of cardinals in the dogwood.
With the light in it the dogwood
Seemed to want to make a rhyme.

A Bad Spring

Every night I dose myself:
Here, angel, take this pill and sleep.

Every morning here I am.

We stretch and go outside.
The sky shakes and streaks, the trees
Are a rainbow of green.
All the colors of the green-bow.

Weeping willow, dogwood, questions about real estate,
Unanswerable azaleas in several shades.
I don't know if they grow native here.
I don't know my credit score, the date of my last period,
Any other logistics.
I push those sorts of questions to the side.

Pollen piles on the mailbox.
In the mailbox they announce they're not bills yet,
But bills they will be soon. Not all mine.

Every day I call myself:
Here, angel. Or not that. Through emptiness

I come running back
On my little feet, ready for breakfast.

Vacation Song

Sorry to interrupt your peace. No it's my job just to sit around soaking up beauty like a sponge. The tall weeds blew in circles, a big gull flew by. Black shards from a campfire. Everybody's thinking there might not be much else left soon. Burnt shards. No everybody's thinking that.

Get it tattooed on your calf or your forearm. The only being on the rocky outcrop, some things present in their outlines while the others sink into the sea. The other things dissolve in toxic fog. The other things are sold in pieces so small you couldn't recognize. Everybody's thinking it. Speculated on all you ever loved. Told to be itself properly or it couldn't exist. We all did it.

The days fell out light and hardwood. We almost didn't recognize it.

But time has a different song about being out of place. Big waves open doors on the beach, the wind shuts them. My voice, it just came out like that. The blond ladies massaging their shiny bony hands around their rings. It's so spectral around here. Are the busboys mocking you. A long time ago I dreamed some lines, and now they're coming true

      are the busboys mocking you
      I dreamed some lines, they're coming true

      it might be
      how the world ends

            the executioner's whistle—

            beautiful color—

            a shell—

Poem

where has it gone, my booming voice
I wanted to take it with me through the streets

where has it gone, the train I took
I wanted to lie down in the sharp snowy sticks

see how each line demonstrates the subjunctive
"I wished I were somewhere other than"

that a willow tree might be recovered
from remembering the real structure of place

the lime-green leaves

that it might be a long day without spectacle
in the teeth of the forces we made

some room for the seasons we knew waiting out the year
with a phone charger a parking space somewhere to stash your dog while you wait

crossing the coasts to the other one often
waiting at the light while the sky went terrifically blank
waiting for the light when the first bird starts like a social ghost

Song of Untellable Distances

Like a rope with nothing to be tied to: to delegate process to a higher power but not higher, pollen chilled to yellow, splish-splash like the turtles off the tree branch in the shallows. Oh perfect voice, will you tell the truth about our wheat? Tie me to whatever breeze is shaping our things in the windless galley. What befell you after the giant smoking O's? Intoxication in whatever sense. When the bird stops, write a letter, write a letter every time the bird stops until you spell our death, all of us. Untell it till we're talking only about animals and the air. The turtles jumped in the water as soon as I started stepping in the grass—

encounter with paper
roaming charisma
what to do with wasted empty space

subsumption of people
zippered floating individual
someone just drove off in my car

hi love can you hear me
can you hear me now
if there were a truer more projective way—

catastrophe singer
in time to eat dinner
and then we throw our trashy glasses in the sea

The Capitals

In late June in the capitals I slept on different pillowcases
Smelling the detergents they use in the capitals
The question is what do they do to merit living
I mean afford
It is pleasant and the roses growing in the front-yard patches
A big yew tree the nightbirds the elegant streets
The question is who does your money come from
The question is whose loss
The question is whose loves are torn like wet paper for your money
Whose lines are crossed by it
Who can't live the thing she wants which is good and reasonable
Because of your money
The nightbird sings away beside a white row house
Your money makes someone want to work all the time
Turn your other cheek on your clean stripey pillowcase it smells
Like detergent like your door closed to the outside of the capital city
The white roses in the dark green leaves coming up over the red brick wall
It is a garden it is a cycle of toxic violence it grows
Violence or at least nothing to eat, nothing at all

It is a garden whose real lives are distanced
In function of your money
Who among us after all has no pillow
In the evenings they seal themselves up
When the sky turns pink
In the evenings they emerge and laugh
As the sky turns pink
The empty stores are ways for your money to make more of it
When could we emerge into the evening just to be there
For example your money holds multiple people in a space for a while
They could dwell and multiply and need your money
Your money has no border so it makes one where it goes
Otherwise you could pay to drink champagne by the border
In a leather booth beneath the big sky turning pink
In late June it is cold in the capitals but people flock there for the skies
In late June it is cold but people have flocked anyway to make you money
In late June it is cold but your money has gathered all the people there
To make you more
How is it still light out

Whose lives are rubbled Whose rubble Never mind
For your money Whose What is drowned exhausted
Is fished out Is asphyxiated by the air Is slowly
Finished by the air is acid in the water in the food
The money fishing in your toxic money Breathing
In your bed The money till it suffocates Is separated
By your money Is detained by it and for it Is mined
Is killed for

In late June in the capitals I can confirm
Your money is a thing and thriving
Late the late June evening and the sky turns pink
Jasmine the white roses some purple things I don't know how to name
In the capitals one day will your money fall silent
Ever and the bird who sings at night will sing
In the capitals your money rising and the roses
The rubble the stores and everything is brimming full

Accomplice

ACCOMPLICE: wake up
wake up from your dream worlds
your pillows smell like bad hay and city
maybe it's the middle of your life

Even the sky exists
at a remove

What will fill the space between the middle of the night
and the middle of the morning

What do you have
what do you have for it
gummy bear or little pill
musical key or new formal trick

ACCOMPLICE is silent
someone walks by outside

then: rotten to the fucking core
and out the other side

Latin without Latin
salt without salt
these things that were basic for all you boys
in lines—

Music without design
heat without heat
some things that should warn the girls
how time wraps up—

He looked up the rue Frémicourt on the map
and was happy to find it like a bird sailing over Paris

Questions:

The mallard the gull-like plover
or the little grackles by the Seine

Also what it is to sail over

Is it good to be several floors up in the dead of night
is it

Is it a joke

Latin without Latin
salt without salt
heat without heat
fuel without fuel
friends without betraying friends

Is it a theory of aesthetics will it hold water

Will it hold in the morning
while the birds fly over and find what they need

Will they find what they need or won't they

Latin without Latin
salt without salt
heat without heat
fuel without fuel
friends without betraying friends
friends without betraying anyone
friendship without even trying
the long dusty hallway in the dead of night
age without gender
care without what uses up
spring without bug noises throbbing
summer with only mosquitoes from the trash cans, could you
imagine, summer without worry
their faces without bone structure
the ducks landing on the brown dead water anyway
walking without money
friendship without money
money without death without the deaths of anyone
money without death

ACKNOWLEDGMENTS

The epigraph to this book comes from C. D. Wright's essay "Frank Stanford of the Mulberry Family: An Arkansas Epilogue," published in *Conjunctions* (no. 29 [1997]: 297).

The phrase "is this when the poem appears like a crime scene" comes from a talk given by the poet and art historian Jennifer Nelson and is used with admiration and gratitude.

I am so grateful to the editors of the publications in which poems from this book previously appeared:

Alienocene: "Song of Untellable Distances"
Bennington Review: "Poem" (as "Poem for the New Year")
Berkeley Poetry Review: "The Upstate" (two poems) and "Just Work"
Company: "Song of Accumulation" and "Accomplice"
Dusie Tuesday poem series: "Forms of Displeasure"
Jubilat: "Planning"
Lana Turner Journal: "Vows"
Rob McLennan's *Medium* Spotlight series: "New City"
Ocean State Review: "Accomplice (Isabella from *Measure for Measure*)" and "A Bad Spring"
Oversound: "Dogwood" and "Tennessee Quatrains"
Prelude: "Accomplice" and "The Upstate" (as "untitled: 2/1/17")
Stinging Fly (Ireland): "Tender Publics" and "Charm for G"
The Volta: "Pretty Like That," "Wasted Empty Space," and "The Capitals"

A tremendous thank you to Srikanth Reddy, Rosa Alcalá, Douglas Kearney, and Katie Peterson—and to everyone at the University of Chicago Press—for seeing this book and making it a better one.

Deepest thanks to my friends, family, and teachers for love, wisdom, and sustenance. Thank you to everyone who read at or came to a Small House Poetry Reading in Greenville, South Carolina, between 2016 and 2018—you kept this writing alive. Thank you to Sadie the dog, and thank you always to Walt.